Relight the Fire!

How You Can Win Souls and Do Outreaches

DEBRA GEORGE

RELIGHT THE FIRE
How You Can Win Souls and Do Outreaches

Copyright © 2012 by Debra George

ISBN 978-1-4675-6375-8

debrageorgeministries@gmail.com
www.debrageorge.org

Published by Rozetta's Graphics - 409-225-5445
rozetta@sugarlandgraphics.com

ACKNOWLEDGEMENTS

HANDS DOWN I am GRATEFUL to my brother in law and sister, Richard and Tena Ford, who are the wonderful Pastors of Family Worship Center in Stafford, Texas. Tena led me to Christ when I was a wild partying college student. Both Richard and Tena taught me God's Word, discipled me and believed in me. I had the honor of walking along beside the two of them for many years where I learned about the ways and things of God. Because of these two great people I am graced by God to minister all over the world today.

INTRODUCTION

God wants to use you to be one of his AMAZING SOUL WINNERS. No matter what your background is, what side of the tracks you grew up on or what your present condition or circumstances are, God WANTS TO USE YOU! On the inside of you, there is greatness and it is WAITING to come out. Even before you were ever formed in your Mother's womb, God knew you and He approved of you. (Jeremiah 1:5). It is God's very best plan for us to reach out and to tell the untold about the love of Jesus Christ.

On the inside of every born again child of God is a desire... a desire to bring others to Jesus Christ.

Since our desires are connected to our destiny, then it is part of God's great plan and DESTINY for us to WIN SOULS!

I meet and talk with believers all of the time who want to win souls, who want to make a difference, but just don't know how. I meet Pastors and church leaders who want to start a great outreach through their local churches, but they need the right person to help them get it started. Many times in our local churches, the staff is already maxed out taking care of the important day to day needs that every church has. I have had Pastors share with me that they simply don't have the finances to outreach into their city.

Today I want to encourage you and show you how you can have a powerful outreach with a minimal amount of people, time and finances. That's what this book is all about, "OUT-REACH MADE SIMPLE." Whatever city, town, country or state you live in, you can start an outreach and it's simple. Come on! Let's get started and I will show you how.

"…He who wins souls is wise."

Proverbs 11:30

Chapter One
CAN ONE PERSON MAKE A DIFFERENCE?
YOU CAN!

Born again as a young 20 year old college student as my Sister led me to Jesus in the living room of her home in Sugar Land, Texas; I immediately began to tell others about Christ. My Sister, Tena Ford, is a powerful soul winner. Every time I was with her, she was always leading someone to Jesus, handing out Gospel tracts and giving words of hope and encouragement. It wasn't long before I was winning souls myself. Why? Because I got around another soul winner. When we get around someone who is winning souls, the fire and anointing that is on their life will begin to rub off on us and that's exactly what happened to me.

Soul winning is addicting! Whether it's a cashier at a department store, a fellow class mate, or a stranger walking down the street, I began to share God's love wherever I went and He began to save the lost and hurting.

When I approach someone to witness to them, I always tell them that Jesus loves them. I then ask them if they have Jesus living in their heart......and then I ask the BIG QUESTION, "Are you sure you are going to Heaven?" Many times people respond with a "no" or "I don't know" or "I sure hope so." I then say, "Well let's take care of that right now. Grab my hand and in 60 seconds or less, you will be sure that Jesus lives inside of you and that you are on your way to Heaven." I rarely ever get turned down, but if I do, I keep on moving knowing that the seed of God's love and His Word are planted in the heart of those we witness to. His Word never returns or comes back void. (Isaiah 55:11).

Marketplace ministry is one of the greatest ministries on earth. Jesus said in Mark 16:15 that we are to go into all the world and preach the Gospel. I believe what Jesus is saying to us today is that we are to go into OUR WORLD, the world we live in, the people we see each day and share God's love with them.

Whether it's the classmate who has a locker next to you, a co-worker, or your next-door neighbor, everyone needs Jesus!

Today wherever you are located geographically is the place where God wants to use you. I heard T. L. Osborne say one time that your hometown is the proofing ground for your ministry. There's no accident that you live where you live, so let's allow God to use us to the fullest right where we are!

Chapter Two
SOUL WINNING IS FOR YOU

If you want to become a **soul winner,** you have to recognize that **soul winning is for right now and that soul winning is for you!** The Bible says in II Corinthians 6:2, "I have heard you in a time accepted, and in the day of salvation have I succoured you: behold, now is the accepted time; behold, now is the day of salvation." Jesus wants you and me to know that in order to become a soul winner, we have to recognize that soul winning is for right now and soul winning is for you. Jesus wants us to know that **we can become a soul winner.**

A number of years ago my whole life changed for the better. Suddenly one night as I was sitting in my living room, Jesus walked into my room and He visited me. I didn't see Jesus, although I understand that this has happened to other people. However, I knew when He came into my one bedroom pink apartment, for His presence filled the place. He said to me that night, "Debra, I've called you to be a soul winner and from this moment forward, **the anointing that I've placed upon your life to win the lost is about to intensify.**" I was excited, but I did not realize at that moment, the impact of everything that Jesus was telling me would change my life forever.

The following evening after this great visitation, I was returning from the grocery store at about 10:00 p.m. when I recognized a young man named Steven who was walking along the side of the street. I knew Steven from the grocery store and also from my local church. I pulled my car over and offered him a ride home which he gladly accepted. When I asked him where he lived, I realized that he lived in an apartment complex that was filled with drugs, violence, and crime. I thought to myself, "This is not a safe place for a woman to be driving at this time of the night. However, after Steven got out of my car and said goodbye, I pulled my car into a dark alley way, which was the only place to turn around. As I pulled into the alley, I noticed about sixteen teenagers. Some of them were playing basketball and others were hitting a volleyball around. They did not seem to be too happy with me for interrupting their game to turn my car around.

I was somewhat relieved as I was driving away from the apartment complex when suddenly the Holy Spirit spoke down deep in my spirit and said, "Debra, turn your car around, go back down the alley way and preach Jesus to those teenagers." I was amazed that God would require something so radical from a woman like me alone in the middle of the night. I thought to myself, "How could I be qualified to preach to teenagers in the middle of the night?" However, God chooses the foolish things of this world to confound the wise. (I Corinthians 1:27). Remember in the book of I Samuel how God told Samuel to anoint David as king. He was the most unlikely person to ever be used by God, but we all know what a mighty servant of the Lord David became. This is a perfect illustration of how God has chosen you and me to be used in His Kingdom to become great soul winners to our families and to the world around us.

On this particular night, **God's voice was like a gentle tapping on the shoulder** or a passing thought that said, "Go and preach to those teenagers." I knew beyond a shadow of a doubt that the voice I heard was God's voice because when the Holy Spirit speaks to us, **His voice and His commands will always bring glory to Jesus.** (John 16:14). As I turned my car around in order to obey God, my flesh was dying a thousand deaths. I could not believe that God could use such an ordinary person to do something so extraordinary in His Kingdom.

As I drove into the alley way for the second time, I got out of my car, turned my ignition and headlights off, and walked right into the middle of the teenager's volleyball and basketball games. I cleared my throat, paused for a moment and then I said, "Can I have your attention for just a moment, please?" As I looked up, a huge guy was staring down at me dribbling a basketball as I silently prayed, "Oh, Lord, let him like me." I knew that if he didn't, that this big, burly guy could smash me into the ground in a second flat! As I waited for his response, he said "Okay." After I took a deep breath, I proceeded.

By this time I had the attention of the whole group, JUST AS GOD HAD PLANNED! I said to the teens, "I normally do not come down dark alley ways in the middle of the night, however, GOD SENT ME HERE." Now if you ever tell anyone that God has sent you, they will listen to you simply because they think you're crazy. This was probably the case with them!

I went on to preach MY FIRST ALLEY WAY SERMON. I said, "Jesus loves you. You are so very special to Him. He died for you and wants you to spend eternity in Heaven with Him. You can be one hundred percent sure tonight that you will spend eternity in Heaven. Can I join hands and pray with you to receive Jesus into your heart as your Savior?" They said, "Yeah, that will be alright." As we were about to pray, one of the teenager's mother, who was standing several yards behind me, yelled out with a loud voice, "Don't start praying without me. I want to make sure I'm going to Heaven, too." Then she ran over to the circle of teens and grabbed hands and prayed with us.

I rejoiced as I left the alley way that night because approximately sixteen teens and one little mother had been BORN AGAIN BY THE SPIRIT OF GOD! HIS CALLING ON ME TO WIN SOULS WAS JUST BEGINNING.

In the next few days that followed, a young man at a local swimming pool was born again. As I walked past him I heard Jesus say,

"I want to save him now," and He did! A woman at the dry cleaners was saved. A man at the racquetball court who was involved in a cult was saved. Two maintenance men who worked in my apartment complex were riding on their golf cart whenever the Holy Spirit hit me. I jumped onto the golf cart with them, preached Jesus Christ to the two of them and they prayed with me to be saved! What an awesome God we serve!

A soul winning fire had begun to burn within me, an unquenchable fire that cannot be put out. The Bible says in Hebrews 1:7 that *"...HIS MINISTERS ARE A FLAME OF FIRE."* What a glorious thing it is to lead a wandering soul into the Kingdom of Heaven. It is surely the highest calling in the church today to obey Jesus' great commission, "Go into all the world and preach the Gospel to every creature." (Mark 16:15). Go ahead and become one of God's overnight soul winners. Jump on a golf cart or two. Witness at the cleaners or the grocery store. Snatch someone out of darkness. Do something!

The Bible says in Matthew 11:12, "And from the days of John the Baptist until now the Kingdom of heaven suffers violence, and the violent take it by force." Let's you and I snatch some folks out of Hell and into Heaven. **You can become a soul winner!** God has incredible assignments just for you. No one can do what you can do in God's Kingdom. It's time for all of us to roll up our sleeves, so to speak, and make a difference in someone's life.

Chapter 3
BEFORE YOU REACH OUT, CRY OUT!

A cry is powerful. Have you ever been in a store or on an airplane and suddenly a baby begins to cry at the top of their lungs? Not only can you not help but hear the cry, you usually turn around to see where the cry is coming from.

That's how God feels about you and me. He hears your cry! When you cry out, He turns to look! He pays attention and listens to what you are crying about! I am reminded of the story of a blind man in the Bible named Bartimeaus. As he sat by the roadside begging, he heard that Jesus was passing by. This man without shame, right in front of his friends, family and everyone who knew him began to cry out. He cried out for Jesus to have mercy on him. He didn't cry out once and quit. He didn't cry out twice and decide to give up.

Even when his friends told him to be quiet, he screamed out all the louder. He got the attention of Jesus! Suddenly Jesus stopped, called the man over to him and he received his sight! Friends, if this man would have listened to everyone else that day, he would still be blind. However, he went against the tide. He went against the norm. He broke out of his box and he cried out to God! Something supernatural happens when we cry out. The ears of the Lord are open to the cry of the righteous. (Psalm 34:15).

I can remember a season in my own personal life where I became DESPERATE....DESPERATE to win more souls for Jesus than ever before. I had always been a soul winner, but I desired MORE....MUCH MORE! Life happens to all of us and it doesn't matter who we are. Jesus said that we would have tribulation or trouble in the world but that we are to be of good cheer because He has already overcome every thing we will be faced with. (John

16:33). I remember like it was yesterday going through the pain of an unwanted divorce. I remember when my Dad went home to be with the Lord. I remember spending lots of extra time with my Mom because we needed each other more than ever. I can also remember the day when I discovered that I just wasn't ON FIRE for God like I was at one time. I remember talking to a couple of friends about my DESIRE to win more souls. I remember them asking me a great question, "What are you going to do about it?" I looked at my two friends and I said, "I don't know, but something!"

And something, I did. It wasn't long after this that I began to watch Paula White on television. I was moved by the clips they showed of her in the inner city winning souls and helping hurting humanity. Night after night I knelt in front of my television set, placed my hands on the screen and said, "God use me to win more souls the way you are using this great woman." Shortly after that I went to hear a speaker by the name of Darlene Bishop at our friend's church, Maranatha, in Mont Belvieu, Texas. All of five feet tall, Darlene spoke of the FIRE OF GOD and how God wants each of us to VOICE our DESIRES to HIM.

In August of 2005, I left the conference with a new zeal and determination to get a hold of God concerning my DESIRE to win more SOULS! Night after night at 8 PM, I turned off everything… no television, no phone calls, no nothing! I went to my bedroom, got down on my hands and knees before God and prayed a three word prayer that forever changed my life, "RELIGHT THE FIRE."

Night after night, I cried out to God to allow me to win more souls. I told Jesus over and over again that I wanted to win a lot of souls and I was asking Him to lead me to them. That was in August of 2005. I continued to pray, "RELIGHT THE FIRE" God.

It was September and not much was changing, so I thought. Looking back on this time now, I realize that God was drawing me closer to have a more intimate relationship with Him. September passed and now it was October, still I refused to give up or to let go. I would say things like, "God you know where all of the souls are, I don't. I am trusting you to lead me to them. RELIGHT THE FIRE."

Now it was December and still I refused to quit! Night after night I cried out to God to "Relight The Fire." October passed, now it was November. With a towel on my bedroom floor and my face buried in it, night after night, I cried out! Still it didn't look like much was happening. But after all, we don't go by what we see. II Corinthians 5:7 says, "We walk by faith and not by sight." Now it was December and still night after night I cried out.

One morning I got dressed and drove to Columbus, Texas where I had the honor of teaching 200 plus young people at Texas Bible Institute for my dear friends, Tommy and Rachel Burchfield. We had an awesome time in the presence of God and as I drove away from Columbus, Texas that day, I had NO IDEA that God was going to move in a way that would change my life forever! I was about to find out that God honors us when we pour our hearts out to Him. "Relight the Fire!"

Chapter 4
THE DIFFERENCE ONE ACT
OF OBEDIENCE CAN MAKE!

It seemed like "just another day" when I pulled into Larry's Mexican Restaurant in Richmond, Texas on my way home from Columbus. I wanted to take one last look at their party room where I would surprise my Sister for her birthday. As I got out of the car, I noticed two women standing in the parking lot. God spoke to me deep down in my spirit saying, "Tell those ladies about me. They will be saved today." As I started walking toward them, I could not help but laugh because one of the ladies was wearing a T-shirt that said, "Beer, Beads and some other words." What a perfect candidate to meet Jesus Christ, I thought. As I began talking to the ladies, I found out pretty quickly that they did not know anything about having a personal relationship with Jesus Christ. We prayed together right then as both of them, Benita and Juanita asked God to forgive them of their sins and invited Jesus Christ to come and live in their heart.

I was so excited that I ran to my car, grabbed a scratch piece of paper, jotted down my cell number and said to the two of them, "If you ever need anything, call me." I never dreamed in a million years that they would call, but several days later, they did. Benita asked me to meet her at the same place in the parking lot the next day at 11 AM. I agreed to go. The next day as I drove into the restaurant, there stood Benita. I got out of the car and she walked up to me and hugged me and said, "Debra I love you and today I am giving my whole life over to God. Whatever happened to me the other day, please go tell my Sister and her children. They are sitting across the parking lot in a van." As I approached the van, Benita introduced me to her Sister, Cookie. She and her children prayed with me to be saved that day also! Wow, look at what God is doing. But what I did not know is that we were just getting started. Benita then asked me to get into my car and follow them across the railroad tracks so they could show me where they lived. I agreed. As I drove through her neighborhood, I saw the people and I saw their great needs.

For the next few weeks, I began to walk the streets of Benita's inner city neighborhood. Many times she would be with me. With a bag of candy in my hands, I witnessed to children, teenagers, drug dealers, prostitutes, you name it, about Jesus Christ. In a few short weeks, about 100 people had received Him as their Savior!

I didn't know much about Benita or Juanita, but it wasn't long until I found out that Benita was a crack addict and a prostitute and Juanita was alcoholic and homeless sleeping on the ground behind the very restaurant where we prayed. Benita knew everyone and she quickly made sure that I met and prayed with everyone she knew.

A lot of times we think we need a big Bible, the right kind of clothes to wear or to memorize a few more scriptures before we win souls. All I needed was one good hooker to reach the people of the inner city. She was the key that unlocked an entire region for the glory of God to visit. It wasn't long before I gathered up my friends, I got my posse together so to speak and we began to take our cars into their neighborhood picking them up and bringing them to church. Children, teens, drug addicts, alcoholics and people from all walks of life piled in our cars week after week to go to the house of God, a great church in Stafford, Texas; Family Worship Center. The harvest became so great that this incredible church now sends a bus into this neighborhood every week to bring these beautiful people to church. Their lives continue to be impacted and changed because of the great ministry of Pastors Richard and Tena Ford.

The day I met Benita and Juanita, all I could see were two ladies who gave their hearts to Jesus Christ. But God saw something much greater. He saw many souls that would come into His Kingdom because of one encounter in the parking lot of Larry's Mexican Restaurant. Yes, that's right. We see one thing and God sees another. Two souls became many souls and the harvest continues to be won in the inner city of Richmond, Texas. Can one person make a difference? I am and you can too. Get started right now. Come on and I will tell you how.

Chapter 5
YOU CAN BRING IN THE HARVEST

John 4:35 says, "Do not say there are four months and then comes the harvest, lift up your eyes, look on the fields for they are white already to harvest." God wants to use you to bring a harvest of souls into His kingdom.

I believe because I cried out to God, I met Benita and Juanita who opened up their inner city area to me called, "Mud Alley." It was named this because of all of the prostitution and crack in the area. Since then we have renamed it "Jesus Alley" because of the many lives that are being changed by the power of God's love!

It wasn't long after I met Benita and Juanita in December of 2005, that it was time for Christmas. "I NEED TOYS!" I thought. I ran out to the store, bought a bunch of toys and took them out to Richmond, Texas to start giving away to the children. A few of my friends jumped in and helped me. Many times we would pull up on a street, yell "FREE TOYS!" and the rest was history. The children and the parents would come running. We always prayed with them first to receive Jesus, then last of all we gave away the toys. Other times, we would pull up into the neighbor-hood with tons of clothes that people had given us. We would pile the clothes a mile high at the end of a street called George where the Richmond revival started. We would then go door to door telling everyone that we had free clothes to give away. The people would start coming from everywhere. We gathered them in a small vacant area and shared John 3:16 with them, prayed for salvation and then began to pray for their needs. The power of God was present every time!

The power of God hit one woman and she crumbled, falling on the pavement of the street, shaking because of the power of God.

Some of the people at the outreach gasped, exclaiming that she was dead. I said, "No, she's not dead, this is the power of God!" When we were through praying, we would let them take as many of the clothes as they wanted. It could get pretty heated in the inner city whenever more than one person wanted the same shirt, but we were having fun!

This same day, a woman by the name of Martha invited us into her home. She said she knew God was real because when we were praying outdoors that day, the dark clouds in the sky began to swirl and rumble back and forth in an unusual way. I never saw this phenomenon, but many of the residents attending the outreach sensed God was present because of this wonder. It was supposed to rain that day, but not a drop of rain came until our outreach was over. To Martha, this was a sign that God was real. As we went into her home, all of her family gave their hearts to Jesus and were filled with the Holy Spirit. It was a glorious day indeed!

I call this RAW EVANGELISM. I tell everyone who goes out on the streets with us that it is "ORGANIZED CHAOS." In other words, we can't predict what will happen on the streets. We take giveaways and bless the people as much as we possibly can and we leave the rest up to God. We trust Him to move on our behalf.

Since this day, our outreaches have become a lot more organized, but still have the same powerful impact. We now set up all of our giveaways on tables, serve refreshments, go in a day early and hand out flyers thus reaching a larger percentage of the area by doing so.

Many times we want to SAVE THE WORLD in a day, but with outreach, I encourage you to target an area. Drive through or walk through a neighborhood. Begin to pray and trust God to make a difference in one region. When you take the first step of faith, God will help you by showing you what your next step will be. Remember how I got started on the streets winning more souls. I started with a BIG BAG OF CANDY, A BIG GOD, AND A BIG DREAM to win the inner city. When I took the FIRST STEP to start an outreach, God helped me take the REST OF THE STEPS. Zechariah 4:10 says, "Does anyone dare despise this day of small beginnings?" When you start, God will be right there with you to help you along your journey. What He did for me He will do the same for you! All God is looking for is a willing vessel. Are you ready to take the first step? Let's go!

Chapter 6
TAKE A STEP OF FAITH

When you step out by faith and make a decision that you are going to reach out, get ready for God to back you up. Supernatural things will begin to happen for you!

In December of 2011, it was getting close to Christmas and Lakewood Church along with our ministry was collecting a ton of toys to bring to children in the inner city. God gave me an idea to call the outreach, "Circle The City With Toys." I wanted us to bring toys to where the children really needed them in the Houston area. At the same time I wanted to try and find a place that was not too far from Lakewood so we would have a better chance of getting new converts and families into the church.

I was speaking to my friend, Joyce Kahleh, Outreach Director of Lakewood about where we should bring the toys. She asked me to find a place and I said that I would. Late one afternoon, I put my dog, Molly in the car and off we drove. I was driving down 59 North in Houston when I prayed a short simple prayer, "God you know where the children are who need toys. Lead me to them." I drove a distance and I remember as clear as if it were yesterday, the Holy Spirit said, "Exit here." I looked up and the exit sign said Kelley/Cavalcade. In obedience to God I took the exit, turned into a neighborhood, took a left and there I saw a man standing in front of his house near the street. I stopped, put my car window down and said, "Hi I'm Debra George. Lakewood Church in Houston has donated a lot of toys. We would like to bring toys to the children in this area." He responded by telling me that there were a lot of children in the area and that it would be great if we came. I felt so comfortable with this man that I got out of my car and we talked for a few more moments. I found out his name was Alfred. He said we could walk down the street and he would get permission to use a vacant lot for us to park our vehicles when we came. Not only that but Alfred immediately called his best friend, Arthur, who lived a couple of streets over and we were able to see another vacant lot where we could have the outreach. Within 5 minutes, our inner city outreach was planned! I put my two newfound friend's phone numbers in my phone and said I will call you soon. I told them that we will come out several days before the outreach to hand out flyers letting the families know we will be coming to give away free toys. They were excited and so was I!

Before I drove away, I looked up at Alfred and Arthur and asked, "What area of town is this?" They said, "You are in the Fifth Ward." I said, "Oh okay!" Later on I found out that this area was the most dangerous, high crime area in our city. Even most residents don't go outside of their home after dark. The area was more commonly called, "Bloody Fifth" because of all of the murders that occur in this area. I thought, "Wow God, you know what you are doing!" I left feeling like God, Molly, and me had hit the jackpot!

When I was about to leave, I glanced down at my phone where someone had written on my facebook that there were children in Houston at I 10 East and Freeport Exit that needed toys. I drove on to I-10 and took the Freeport exit and turned down a street. I saw hundreds of people standing everywhere and there were dancers in costumes standing at the end of the street. I parked my car, got out and went and met the dancers. They were celebrating a holiday and I had a captive audience. I immediately began to talk to the people who lined the streets letting them know that we wanted to come to their area with free toys for the children. I noticed one woman standing nearby and I walked up to her and shared what Lakewood Church wanted to do. In moments, I found out that she lived on that very street in an apartment. She said that she knew the apartment manager and would get permission for us to come onto the parking lot of their complex to have our Christmas Outreach. I put the woman's number in my phone and told her we would be coming several days before the outreach to hand out flyers. Within 10 minutes, Houston Outreach #2 was planned! We were ready to circle the city with toys on behalf of Pastors Joel and Victoria Osteen.

Whenever you set your heart for God to use you in a great way, He will be with you and He will open up the right door.

When the day of the outreach came, we drove up to Fifth Ward where about 150 to 175 people were already waiting in line for us! Many were saved, healed, delivered and set free. We had so much fun giving toys to the children and we even served everyone cake and drinks as they waited in line! What an amazing God we serve! We ran out of toys and had about 20 children left. We explained to the families that we had another stop to make and that we would be back at about 4 PM with more toys.

Off we went to I-10 East apartments where about 100 people were waiting on us. They received Jesus and were blessed with toys! As we got into our vehicles to head back over to Fifth Ward, some friends of ours had already gone out to the store to purchase more toys. We were about to drive off when it began to pour down rain. I never thought in a million years that families would be waiting for us in Fifth Ward. First of all we were running about 2 hours behind. Second of all it was raining. We drove straight to the outreach location in Fifth Ward in the rain and there stood children and their parents on the vacant lot in the pouring rain. Our hearts were so touched. As we got out of our vehicles, one woman said to me, "I didn't think you would come back." I said, "If we say we are coming back, then we are coming back." In the pouring rain, we handed out the rest of the toys making sure every child received a gift. I remember one little boy running his fingers on the outside threading of a football and saying to his Mom, "Look

Mom, this is a REAL FOOTBALL." We were brought to tears of joy over the souls that were saved and the children that were blessed!

The Osteen family has started declaring that this area is called, "Blessed Fifth" instead of "Bloody Fifth."

All God wants is someone who is willing. Step out and believe God for the supernatural! Friends, our words have creative power. Use your words and prayers to turn your area around for the glory of God!

Chapter 7
BEING CONSISTENT WITH YOUR FIRE

It's REAL EASY to get on fire for God! It's quite another thing to STAY ON FIRE! Many times life has a way of pulling us down. Just when we think we are on fire and on top of our world, someone or something comes along with a big, fat water hose to try to extinguish our fire. Life's tough circumstances unfortunately usually come blow after blow leaving us staggering, reeling and trying desperately to make it through the day. Life's distractions can get us off course so quickly to the point that days, weeks, months and even sometimes years can go by until we realize that we are not as "on fire" as we could be. This is the time to make a change, to make a note to self that says something like, "NO MATTER WHAT TODAY BRINGS, I WILL REMAIN CONSISTENTLY ON FIRE FOR MY GOD!" Apostle Paul reminds Timothy about the importance of God's fire in II Timothy 1:6, "That is why I would remind you to stir up (rekindle the embers of, fan the flame of, and keep burning) the [gracious] gift of God, [the inner fire]…"

On the inside of each of us lies the gracious gift of God, an inner fire. It's up to us to fan the flame. When the trials of life broadside us, many times we feel like our fire for God is gone. But thank God it's not. Beneath where the fire used to burn strong and bright lies the embers when once stirred immediately comes back to life! Sometimes all we need is for the right person to come along and throw a little gasoline on our fire to get it burning bright once again!

In the winning of souls and doing outreaches, there's nothing that can be more important than staying consistent with the fire God has given you. I was on top of the world when God supernaturally led me to Houston's Fifth Ward.

OUTREACH ON THE STREETS
FAMILY WORSHIP CENTER
PASTORS RICHARD AND TENA FORD, STAFFORD, TEXAS

HOW IT ALL STARTED

Benita and Juanita saved in parking lot of Larry's Mexican Restaurant in Richmond, Texas. These same gals several days later took me into their neighborhood known as Mud Alley and I began to pass out candy and win souls!

Training Soul Winners At Family Worship Center

Preaching at the end of George Street in Richmond, Texas with Family Worship Center

- 22 -

Souls in the Apartments

Preaching on top of a table in a park

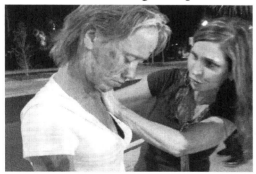

WINNING SOULS IN FLORIDA PROSTITUTION/ CRACK DISTRICT

Precious girl gives
her life to Jesus

WINNING SOULS IN FLORIDA PROSTITUTION/CRACK DISTRICT

Homeless man wanted to end his life, but God

Precious girl shared openly of her addiction to prostitution and drugs

Praying with her for salvation

WINNING SOULS IN FLORIDA
PROSTITUTION/CRACK DISTRICT

MEXIA, TEXAS PARKSIDE CHURCH
PASTORS JARED AND JAMIE ROGERS
Soul winning team in Mexia

SOULS WON IN MEXIA, TEXAS

SOULS WON IN FREEPORT, TEXAS
PASTORS B. F.. AND BRENDA GEORGE

Preaching on tennis courts

Giving toys away

TRAINING TEXAS BIBLE INSTITUTE STUDENTS IN COLUMBUS, TEXAS FOR PASTORS TOMMY AND RACHEL BURCHFIELD

WORLD HARVEST CHURCH, COLUMBUS OHIO
PASTOR ROD PARSLEY

TRAINING SOUL WINNERS

WORLD HARVEST CHURCH COLUMBUS, OHIO
PASTOR ROD PARSLEY

Valor Christian College students on the streets

Souls won in inner city projects

TRAINING SOUL WINNERS TRINITY CHRISTIAN CENTER
ANGLETON, TEXAS - PASTORS GARY AND PENNY LANIER

HANDING OUT FLYERS - HOUSTON, TEXAS

MAN JUST RELEASED FROM PRISON WAS LED TO JESUS WHILE HANDING OUT FLYERS

GIVING AWAY TOYS IN SAN ANTONIO

SOUL WINNING TEAM
FIFTH WARD OUTREACH - LAKEWOOD CHURCH
PASTOR JOEL OSTEEN

Preaching
John 3:16
from the
back of a
pick up
truck

People Line
Streets of
Fifth Ward

FIFTH WARD OUTREACH - LAKEWOOD CHURCH
PASTOR JOEL OSTEEN
People lift their hands to receive Jesus

Cowboy Gives
His Life to Jesus

Rickie Bradford
Sings and Helps Us

Joyce Kahleh
And I Giving
Out Clothes

FIFTH WARD OUTREACH - LAKEWOOD CHURCH
PASTOR JOEL OSTEEN

Kika And Her
New Yellow
And White Dress

Precious boy tells his
Mom, "Look a real
football" as he runs his
fingers across the threading. I will never forget
him!

Giving away bicycles

Man rides his horse
up to outreach and
is born again!

AWESOME FRIENDS WHO LOVE WINNING SOULS

Two Sisters Saved
Cookie and Benita, saved in
Richmond outreach

Alfred, the man I met in Fifth
Ward when I was looking for
a place to give toys away

Setting up tables and getting toys ready for outreach

We love seeing the children blessed at our outreaches

The amazing team from Lakewood Church saw a harvest of souls come into God's Kingdom. Though, it was exciting to see 150-175 souls born again, we weren't finished. In fact, we were just getting started in the Fifth Ward. Seven months later, we went back into the area with a team and handed out bags of much needed toiletry items. Many were saved on this day! We then began to make plans to go back during the month of December and hand out toys to the children. Little did I know that God was about to more than double the harvest that we had seen a year earlier.

When we began to hand out flyers in Fifth Ward the day before our outreach, God moved! Right off the bat, we approached a man who shared with us how he had just gotten out of prison and lived on the streets. He explained to us how he could never accept Jesus Christ because of all of the wrong he had done. Within minutes, I sat down beside him on some rusty steps outside of a store. It wasn't long before his eyes filled with tears. It was obvious to us that God's love was breaking through. I grabbed his hand and he prayed with us inviting Jesus Christ into his heart to save him. He managed to muster up a faint smile as he told us that he couldn't remember the last time he smiled or laughed. He may not have laughed out loud that day but I couldn't help but picture our God laughing right in the face of the enemy that one more precious soul had been snatched out of his grip!

As we continued handing out flyers, I met another man sitting on his front porch with a cowboy hat on. I shared with him about our outreach the next day and asked him his name. He said, "You can call me Cowboy!" I said, "Alright Cowboy, I hope to see you tomorrow." I noticed the empty bottle of Whiskey sitting next to him and his full can of brew that he was sipping on. Right before I walked away, he grabbed my hand and said, "You can't go yet. I won't let go of your hand until you pray for me." And pray for Cowboy we did! As we continued handing out flyers, we managed to converge on the street right in front of an elementary school just as school was dismissing. I got so excited and was telling our team that we hit the jackpot as we started talking to parents and children about coming to the outreach. One of our team members couldn't believe that I was excited about more people coming to our outreach when she knew the number of toys that were donated couldn't possibly take care of the hundreds of children that we handed flyers to. But God had a plan!

I usually don't get much sleep the week of an outreach. I realize first hand that we are going into an area where darkness, sin and crime have tried to prevail and with everything in me, I pray and come against the powers of darkness and trust God for souls to be won, captives to be set free and for our precious teams of volunteers to be safe. Even when we are handing out flyers, I pray constantly and declare that the blood of Jesus Christ and the angels of God surround the region. Prayer works!

The morning of the outreach came. I rode with a good friend of mine, Charles, and he was kind enough to load our sound system and you name it into his truck. As we were en route early that morning we received a call from one of our team members stating that people were already lining up down the street at 7:30 AM for an 11 AM Outreach. "Woo Hoo!!! Here we go!" I thought. Got get em' Jesus!!! I was already so HIGH on the very thought of what JESUS could and would do, I could hardly contain myself.

As we pulled up to the outreach location, and I saw the people lining up, the excitement rushed in on me. I do anything from laughing hysterically to crying spontaneously over the JOY of seeing our GOD answer prayer for the souls of mankind. Set up 101 begins when we run an extension cord from our sound system on the back of a pick up truck to a house across the street. Outreach takes planning and preparation. We go into the area several days in advance to pray and prepare. Part of our prep work is to find an amazing resident who will let us use their electricity the day of our event. We always do something special for this family to be a blessing to them. Tables are set up. Clothes and shoes donated are unloaded. Toys have been put in big garbage bags pre labeled with boys, girls, or teen items. Volunteers begin arriving. Everyone has a job to do. As people wait in line, part of our team hands them bottle water, candy and cookies. Other parts of the team walk through the line, greeting the people, encouraging them and loving on them.

I was blessed beyond measure to have my good friend, rapper and musician, Rickie Bradford sing two songs. I then jumped up on back of the truck and started sharing about John 3:16. I had an amazing friend from Lakewood, Marcel, translate for me in Spanish. We want to make sure everyone hears the simple Gospel message. I speak for about 3-5 minutes. With outreach, I believe in being brief. Move the outreach along. When you are organized and don't keep the people all day, you accomplish several goals. One is that your volunteers will want to help with the next event because you didn't keep them all day long. Two is that the residents attending will remember how you kept the event fun, upbeat yet meaningful and powerful and they will look forward to your return. Three is that before we give away any toys, we lead everyone in the prayer of salvation. THIS IS THE PRIORITY OF EVERY OUTREACH. While the people are walking through the lines to receive toys and gifts, our team is busy at work, handing out gifts and talking to the people in line about their specific prayer needs. As precious residents are prayed for one on one, we see many signs, wonders and miracles. What an amazing God we serve.

I loved bumping into my friend, Kika! She was saved one year prior at our outreach. She had a story to tell and I couldn't wait to hear it. Kika poured out her heart as she shared of how Jesus changed her life since she prayed with us one year ago. Since her salvation, Kika found a job. After working on her job for months her company increased her hours. Not only that, Kika remembered seeing a yellow and white dress at the outreach a year ago. She came up to me and said how she wanted the dress, I handed it to her, hanger and all and she was so excited. You see this dress had a history. Worn by April Osteen Simons first, Lisa Osteen Comes second and yours truly third, I couldn't have been happier about Kika being number 4! To me this dress represented something special! When the prodigal son returned home his Father put a robe on him. I couldn't help but think when I handed the yellow and white dress to Kika that it possibly represented a new beginning for her life. Thank God, that's exactly what God did for her.

Others at the outreach told us over and over again how they had never experienced such an outpouring of God's love.

One man at the outreach danced in the streets most of the time. I'm not sure what he was high on, but he eventually got high on Jesus as he received Christ as his savior. Our newfound friends Cowboy and the precious man who just got out of prison attended our outreach and they were so blessed! Every child received a toy and just when it looked like we were going to run out of toys, our friend Reggie unloaded a truck load of teddy bears. Every child received a toy or a bear and we had some left over.

As the outreach came to an end, the residents kept coming. Many were led to Christ one on one and for me, I dance in the streets a bit and praise God for all of the 500 plus souls that were won! I figured if I could dance in the clubs high on everything but God before I came to Christ, what in the world would stop me now from dancing in the streets of the inner city HIGH on the MOST HIGH GOD, JESUS CHRIST!

We love the people of Fifth Ward so much and cannot wait to continue to go back into this area to spend time with these precious people over and over again.

When I think back on the day that Molly and I jumped in my car to drive through Houston and find where the children were that needed toys to 700 plus souls later being won in the Fifth Ward, it lets me know that there is always someone waiting on the other side of our smallest act of obedience.

Today's your day to step out and allow God's fire to consume you and to get on others you come into contact with! Get on fire! Stay on fire! Be consistent with your fire! God is looking for someone just like you to step out by faith and trust Him to use you in great ways!

Chapter 8
LET'S PRAY!

Prayer is powerful. Prayer is communicating and talking with your God. I am grateful that we have a God we can talk to. The key to bringing in a harvest of souls is to pray, pray, pray! Here are a few key scriptures that I encourage you to say right out loud everyday:

John 14:14 "Yes I will grant [I myself will do for you] whatever you shall ask in my Name [as representing all that I Am]."

Jeremiah 33:3 "Call to Me and I will answer you and show you great and mighty things, fenced in and hidden, which you do not know."

John 15:7 "If you live in Me [abide vitally united to Me] and My words remain in you and continue to live in your hearts, ask whatever you will, and it shall be done for you."

I John 5:14 "And this is the confidence (the assurance, the privilege of boldness) which we have in Him: [we are sure] that if we ask anything (make any request) according to His will (in agreement with His own plan), He listens to and hears us."

I. Pray For Your Family's Salvation. Make It A Priority (Acts 16:31) "And they answered, Believe in the Lord Jesus Christ give yourself up to Him, take yourself out of your own keeping and entrust yourself into His keeping] and you will be saved, [and this applies both to] you and your household as well." **Father in the name of Jesus** I pray for (insert your family member's names). I pray for their salvation. Thank you Jesus for visiting them and for drawing them to you today. Thank you Father for sending people to them to share about your love. I thank you that your angels and your Holy Spirit are at work in their lives. I boldly declare that not many days from now they will surrender their lives to you and be born again in Jesus name.

II. Pray For Addictions And Strong Holds To Be Broken Over Your Loved Ones (II Corinthians 10:4) "The weapons of our warfare are not carnal, but mighty through God to the pulling down of strong holds." **Pray this prayer for your family and loved ones:** "Father in the name of Jesus I take authority over every spirit and strong hold that has my family bound. I command the enemy to get your hands off of (insert your loved one's names) right now in Jesus name. Addictions, I destroy you. Drugs, alcohol, pornography, wrong relationships, perversion, deception, I command to be destroyed in my loved ones' lives. Father I thank you that my family is coming back to you. Thank you my Father for putting laborers, and believers in their pathway to speak the truth in love to them. I declare today that my family is covered in the blood of Jesus Christ and that your angels my Father have charge over them. Thank you for watching over and protecting my family today in Jesus name. I take authority over the spirits of hopelessness and suicide. I command you to take your hands off of my family. I speak peace and a sound mind to every one of my family members in Jesus name. I declare no accidents, no sickness, no disease, no untimely deaths will come to my family in Jesus name. Thank you my Father that your mighty hand is on every one of my family members. Thank you for visiting them and thank you for setting them free to walk with you and to serve you all the days of their lives in Jesus name."

III. Pray For Lost Souls (John 4:35) "Do not say, It is still four months until harvest time comes? Look! I tell you, raise your eyes and observe the fields and see how they are already white for harvesting."

Pray For Lost Souls On:

    a. Your street
    b. Your neighborhood
    c. Your city
    d. Your school
    e. Your co-workers
    f. Your country
    g. The world

Pray this prayer: "Father today I pray for every person who lives on my **street**. Thank you Holy Spirit for touching them, ministering to them and setting them free in Jesus name. I claim salvation for every child, teen and adult on my street in Jesus name. Thank you Father for moving across my **neighborhood.** Thank you for the angels of God, ministering Spirits, assigned to everyone in my neighborhood, apartment complex, or trailer park. I take authority over accidents, death, destruction, divorce, disease, sickness and abuse in the name of Jesus.

I pull down strongholds of alcohol, drugs, lust, crime, gang activity, hopelessness, suicide, depression, addictions, pornography, and all manner of evil in the name of Jesus. Move across my **city**, oh God. I call souls into your Kingdom.

I pray over the **schools and universities** in my area and I thank you my Father for children and young adults that are rising up to take a stand for you Jesus. I come against violence, school shootings, rape and all manner of evil in our schools in the name of Jesus. I thank you Father for giving students who are believers boldness to speak the truth to others who are lost.

Thank you Father for touching the people I work with everyday in the mighty name of Jesus. I thank you that my boss, supervisor and **co-workers** are coming to know you in a personal way in the name of Jesus. I thank you for giving me great favor with each one of them. Help me Jesus to be a bright shining light for you in a dark world.

I release a soul winning fire and revival of souls to sweep across **America** and around the **world** in Jesus name. I call forth souls! I call forth the harvest in the name of Jesus."

IV. Believe For Divine Appointments (Acts 8:29) "Then the [Holy] Spirit said to Philip, "Go forward and join yourself to this chariot."

I love it when God gives us divine appointments. When Philip saw the man on the chariot, the Holy Spirit let him know to go and talk with him. God opened the man's heart and before you knew it, Philip led him to Jesus and then water baptized him. Wow! If God did this for Philip, friends, He will do it for you too. Every day look for God's divine appointments and listen to His voice. Share the love of Jesus with someone each day. Let God use you in your neighborhood, job, school, at the store, etc. You might say, "How do I pray for someone? What should I say?" Here's a few keys to help you.

I always say, "Jesus loves you. Has anyone ever told you that? God has a great plan for your life. You are so special to Him. Have you ever invited Jesus into your heart? Are you sure you are going to Heaven? (If they are not sure I say, "Can I pray with you? It will only take a second and you can be sure where you are going when you leave this earth.")

Repeat this prayer after me: "Father, forgive me of my sins. Jesus come into my heart and save me today. I give you my life and I thank you that I am your child in Jesus name. Amen."

I remember the day I was in line purchasing items at my favorite store, when suddenly I had the desire to tell the cashier about Jesus. Because there were other customers in line, I hurriedly told the lady about Jesus Christ. When I asked her if she was sure she was going to Heaven, she responded by saying that no one had ever said that to her before. Within seconds, she was ready to grab my hand and pray with me. Before I could even lead her in a prayer, the customer behind me in line said, "Wait a minute! I want to get in on this prayer too!" So Jesus not only saved the cashier that day but the customer behind me in line as well.

It's just that simple friends. The more you step out by faith to tell others about Jesus, the bolder you will become. So go ahead and take the first step. God is with you!

Chapter 9
START AN OUTREACH

It's not hard to start an outreach in your area. In fact outreach can be made simple. There are several things that you will want to do to prepare to have an impact for God in your area.

HOW TO PLAN YOUR OUTREACH

1. **Pray** and ask God which place He desires for you to target in your area for souls.

2. **Drive or walk** around in the vicinity preferably near to your local church to see where the needs are the greatest. There may be an apartment complex, a neighborhood or a trailer park where you can start your first outreach.

3. **In your private prayer** time, begin to pray for the people of this area. Ask God to open their hearts and to give you favor with them.

4. **Begin to collect items to give away** when you go into the designated area that you have chosen. I started with big bags of candy to give to the children. After that we collected clothes. When I became more acquainted with the people I saw that they had basic needs, so we collected soap, shampoo, conditioner, brushes, combs, lotion, toothbrushes, toothpaste, and hair spray and put them in little bags. If it is close to school starting then it's a great idea to collect school supplies. If you are on a limited budget, don't try to buy the whole school supply list at once. Collect pencils. Give pencils and candy away! Other inexpensive items to collect for the children are coloring books, bubbles, kites and most of these items can be purchased at the Dollar Stores!

At Christmas we collect toys for the children. We put the toys in big trash bags and label them. For instance the labels on our bags will say:

Girl's Toys: Infant   Boy's Toys: Infant
Girl's Toys: Ages 4 and up   Boy's Toys: Ages 4 and up
Teenage Girls: Toys   Teenage Boys: Toys

When we have bigger gifts donated, for example, a girl's and a boy's bicycle, we purchase a roll of tickets and do a drawing at the end of the outreach. Be creative!

5. **Have cards or flyers printed up** with your church name, address, phone number, website and service times. This is probably something you already have on hand.

6. **You will need blank index cards and pens** in order to get the people's information so you can follow up on them after the outreach. Some churches/ministries use their Visitor Cards or one of their leaders can take their ipad and input names, addresses, emails and phone numbers.

7. **If you decide to target an apartment complex, go or call in advance** and speak to their manager. Let them know what church you are with and how you are desiring to come one day for a couple of hours to give gifts to the children and families.

8. **Set your outreach date.** Most of the time we do our outreaches on a Saturday morning. Set your date well in advance so you can begin to announce it at your church and invite your friends to help you. On Friday afternoon we go to the outreach area and hand out flyers. We let the residents know that we will be in their area the next day at 11 AM for FREE GIVEAWAYS! We always let them know the exact location of the outreach. For instance: On the Children's

Playground or at the end of Avenue E.

9. **Print flyers.** Here is an example of a flyer that we used at one of our outreaches.

Merry Christmas

+FREE TOYS
FREE BICYCLES +
FREE HAIRCUTS +
FACE PAINTING +

Let's Celebrate Jesus!

This Saturday, Dec.15 @ 11AM
Location: Corner of Brewster &
Retta St.
Bring the Whole Family!
Sponsored by Lakewood Church

10. **Hand out flyers** the day before your outreach.

OUTREACH DAY

On outreach day, the excitement continues. Here's what we do:

1. **Have a Soul Winning Training Session** on the day of your outreach. Meet at your church at 9:30 AM for a brief training session, one hour or less and a time of prayer. In our training session, I go ahead and divide our team into groups. I have taken as few as three on the streets and as many as two hundred. Numbers do not matter.

2. **In our training sessions I encourage everyone with scriptures.** See Chapter 8 on Let's Pray for the scriptures I use. Then we pray down Heaven over the area. Chapter 8 also has specific prayers that we pray and we always pray Psalm 91 over our team and that God's protection will be on us.

3. **Gather your giveaways**, cards or flyers with church information and blank cards and pens to write down contact information of your new friends.

4. **Dress casual.** In the summertime, it's important to stay hydrated. In all of our Summer outreaches, we always bring bottles of water for our team and for the residents.

5. **When we arrive at the outreach location,** there is usually a crowd of people waiting on us. One group unloads the giveaways. Another group lets the residents know where the giveaway line will start so they can begin getting in their place to receive their free gifts. The rest of the team goes to each resident, hugging the children, handing out candy and drinks, meeting the adults and letting them know how much we appreciate them coming.

If you arrive and there is not a group of people waiting on you, do not be discouraged! Take your team door to door inviting everyone to come to the designated spot for FREE GIVEAWAYS in the next five minutes. This is what we say when we go to someone's door: "Hello, my name is Debra George. I am with Life Church and we are here to be a blessing to you and your family today. We are giving away free toys for your children and we have something to give to adults too. We are meeting in five minutes next to the swing set. Come on out and join us."

I encourage teams when going door to door to not go inside of someone's home unless you have a designated leader with you who gives their approval. For instance, there have been occasions when the resident wants us to pray for someone who is sick and unable to come to the door. I have done this many times however I do not recommend this unless you are with one of your Pastors or leaders.

Another important point is that when we knock on doors I always knock and then take a few steps back away from the door and wait for someone to answer. I take teams into the drug districts a lot and you never know what condition the person is in who answers the door. Be waiting and smiling! Use wisdom.

We always have men on the streets with us, however I always keep the women on the forefront and visible for two reasons:

• Women will be more responsive to coming to an outreach with their children when they meet and connect with another woman. In some cases the husband or man of the house will not want his family to attend if he does not see any women on your team. These are suggestions and of course there is an exception to every rule.

• When I take teams into the prostitution district, I use ladies to talk to the prostitutes though men are always present for safety reasons.

6.	**When we start the outreach**, I stand and greet the people and let them know how much we appreciate them coming. I then say, "We are here on behalf of (name of your church and Pastors). We have some free gifts to give you today because we want to be a blessing to you. Before we give you these gifts I want to take one minute of your time and tell you about the GREATEST FREE GIFT you can ever receive, the gift of Jesus Christ, everlasting life. The Bible says in John 3:16 that God so loved YOU, that He gave His only begotten Son, Jesus, that whoever believes on Him should not perish but have everlasting life."

7.	**Pray with the people.**	I want all of you to lift up your right hand like you had a question at school. Now lift up your left hand like you had two questions to ask. This is a sign of surrendering your life to God. Now repeat this prayer out loud after me, "Lord Jesus, forgive me of all of my sins. Come into my heart and save me today. I believe that your blood Jesus washes all of my sins away and that I now am a child of God. Thank you for saving me in Jesus name."

8.	**Announce the name of your church when you finish praying.** Include church location and service times for the next day. Always mention about programs you have for children, teens and adults so that they know you have something for every age. If possible, let the residents know that your team will be coming by in the morning an hour prior to services to pick them up for church.

9. **Pray one on one with the residents.** The next thing I do is tell them that your team is coming by to ask you if you need prayer

for anything special and they will pray with you. If you approach someone and they say that they don't need any prayer, I always ask them if I can pray and ask God to bless them. They usually say yes. Pray short and powerful prayers.

10. **During prayer time, have your team get resident's information written on cards** so that you have a way to follow up on them. You will want to make sure your information cards include their names, children's names and ages, address, phone number and email address. During this time, make sure that you have handed them a card or flyer with your church information on it.

11. **Start giving your items away.** Begin to move the line along and have part of your team stationed at your giveaway area to hand the giveaways to the residents.

12. **Hug and love on all of the people.** Let them know how much you care.

13. **Gather your team** when the outreach is over and thank God for what He is doing in your area. Collect the information cards so you know what doors to knock on to bring people to church the next day.

14. **The last and most important key to having a SUCCESSFUL OUTREACH is CONSISTENCY.** Once you go into an area, stop by again with a few friends the next week and knock on the same doors to say hello. Ask them if there is anything that they need prayer for. Remind them that you will be back on Sunday to pick them up for church. It's not necessary to bring giveaways with you each time. We do giveaways about three times a year. The rest of the time, we talk with the people, learn their names, and begin to build relationships with them.

REMEMBER, THE GOAL OF OUTREACH IS TO SEE PEO-PLE COME TO JESUS AND THEN GET PLUGGED INTO YOUR LOCAL CHURCH WITH GREAT PASTORS WHERE THEIR LIVES CAN BE CHANGED AND TRANSFORMED! Possibly you are in a church that does not have an outreach team. You as an individual can do an outreach in your neighborhood by applying the same principles that I use above. Get a friend to help you and do a local outreach. Start inviting and bringing new converts to church with you. It just takes one person to make a difference and that one person is you. Go! Get started today!

Chapter 10
ASK GOD FOR CREATIVE IDEAS

It's never too late to get started. It's never too late to ask God to give you creative ideas on how to win the lost and help hurting people. For instance in my neighborhood, there are 77 homes. I pray daily for the people who live near me and trust God to move in their lives. One Halloween, I had a thought, an idea. Instead of sitting at home all night while everyone else was out trick or treating, why not go door to door and give out candy in our neighborhood? I grabbed up my friend and neighbor, Cerece, and off we went. As we rang doorbells, we shared with everyone how much Jesus loved them. We then asked if there was anything that we could pray with them about. Three people received Jesus as their Savior. One woman who was hurting walked down her driveway with us sharing about her hardships. We were able to pray with her and encourage her. All the while we were handing out candy to everyone! At the end of the night we were amazed at the great things God did, all because of ONE IDEA!

It's not that we need a lot of GOOD IDEAS, all we need is ONE GOD IDEA. That's exactly what happened to me one day when I was at an area nail salon. With my feet in the water preparing for a pedicure and my nails being filed by a technician, God gave me an idea! He spoke down deep into my spirit and said, "Everyone who works at this nail salon can be saved." Surprised by what He said, I glanced up toward Heaven and said back to Jesus, "How?"

Right then as if I was downloading a document into my computer, God began to download His idea into my spirit. When I was finished with getting my nails done, I approached the owner, Lauren. I said, "Lauren, Christmas is right around the corner. Can I come in one night at closing and give a gift to you and to all of your employees?" I went onto say that in addition to that I wanted to take a moment and share with them about the love of Jesus. Without hesitation, Lauren said, "Yes." We set the date and I left her shop that afternoon on a high!

I shared with my friend, Cerece, what had happened and we went to work. We bought bling, perfume, purses, lotion…you name it. We put the gifts in pretty bags and we were ready. Well, almost ready. We began to pray that God would give us favor and prepare the heart of every lady who worked at the nail salon.

When the night of the event came, we walked into the nail salon. To our surprise, every employee and Lauren were waiting for us at the door. As we walked in, they began to clap and clap and clap! We were so blessed. I took a moment and greeted them. I then shared with them John 3:16 and how very much Jesus loves them. Within moments about 20 employees prayed with us to be born again. We then prayed for all of their special needs that night. At the end of the evening we handed them a beautiful gift bag. Their lives were forever changed and so was ours. It was a night to remember.

It doesn't matter what your background is or your experiences in life. God wants to use you. As we get ready to close, take a moment and ask God to give you an idea on how you can reach more people for Him. He will be faithful to use you for His glory. Something as small as a bag of candy can be used by God to bring in a harvest of souls.

In order to win souls and do outreaches, God took one girl with one bag of candy to take **ONE STEP** to talk to **ONE PERSON** to pray **ONE PRAYER** to win **ONE SOUL** that has turned into thousands of souls being won! God can and will do the same thing for you. All you have to do is take the first step. Let's go! Step, step, step….then keep stepping. You got this friend! God is with you and when you win the lost you take on the VERY HEART OF GOD!

Pray this prayer of SALVATION with me:

Jesus, forgive me of all of my sins. Come into my heart and save me. I give you my life and I thank you that I am saved. I am born again. I am a child of God and I am on my way to Heaven. Thank you Jesus for saving me. Amen.

Pray this prayer to WIN SOULS with me:

Jesus, I give you my life fresh and anew and I ask you to relight the fire of God inside of me. I desire to win more souls. Thank you Jesus for divine appointments each day. Lead me and guide me to the ones who need you, Jesus. Use me to be a bold soul winner in Jesus name. Amen.

Debra George

Debra's upbringing by her parents on the "dusty roads" of Clodine, Texas left an indelible mark on her as she saw first hand how they gave from the little they had to the less fortunate. From the men who were called "bumbs" that jumped from the freight trains and headed to her house for a meal, to watching her folks jump out of bed in the middle of the night to take a neighbor or a stranger to the hospital, Debra's mission is to help people's lives become better....greater.... through the love of Jesus Christ.

Whether Debra is walking the streets of the inner city to talk to a child, a prostitute, a drug dealer or speaking in a church or at a conference, her mandate from God never changes. She has devoted her life to Raising Up A Soul Winning Army For God across the earth by training others to share their faith and to win souls.

Debra is the author of several books: You Can Be An Overnight Soulwinner, Soulwinning Anointing, 13 Things Every Teenager Should Know, Ten Lies About Suicide, When Hurt Won't Stop, and Relight The Fire!"

Debra is a powerful speaker in all types of venues. Her passion is to see people of all ages and backgrounds fulfill their God given destiny.

Debra comes highly recommended by: Pastors Richard and Tena Ford, Pastors Joel and Victoria Osteen, Pastors Rod and Joni Parsley, Jesse and Cathy Duplantis, Dodie Osteen, Pastors Tommy and Rachel Burchfield, Lisa Osteen Comes, Paula White, and Darlene Bishop.

If you would like to contact Debra about speaking in your church or event, you may contact her at:

Debra George Ministries
P. O. Box 721
Stafford, Texas 77497-0721

Phone 281-520-0675

debrageorgeministries@gmail.com
www.debrageorge.org